D0017039

IDYLLS
OF THE KING

NOTES

A Critical Study of Tennyson's Idylls of the King

including
Complete Summary
        and
Selected Examination Questions

By
Robert J. Milch, B.A.
Brooklyn College

Cliff's Notes
I N C O R P O R A T E D
BETHANY STATION • LINCOLN, NEBRASKA 68505

©Copyright 1964
by
C. K. Hillegass
All Rights Reserved
Printed in U.S.A.

INDEX

INDEX

IDYLLS OF THE KING

INTRODUCTION

Alfred, Lord Tennyson was the most important poet of the Victorian period, and his works include some of the finest poetry in the English language. The *Idylls of the King* is one of his best known compositions and has much of lasting value to offer the reader.

In this book you will find a complete summary of Tennyson's *Idylls*, as well as an analytical list of all the characters, an evaluation of the poem's meaning and techniques, a biography of the poet, an account of the Arthurian legend, sample examination questions, and a guide for additional reading. All of these present in concise form the most important facts and ideas you should understand in order to appreciate Tennyson fully.

The *Idylls of the King* deals with an exciting era in English history, and with such fascinating and familiar characters as King Arthur, Guinevere, Sir Lancelot, and the other knights of the Round Table. The poem is difficult in parts, as many worthwhile books are, but reading it will be a rewarding and inspiring experience.

A SUMMARY OF IDYLLS OF THE KING

DEDICATION

These *Idylls* are consecrated in tears, and are dedicated to the memory of one who loved them as if he had seen his own image in them. He was a man who seemed in all his virtues and fine qualities to be none other than Arthur's ideal knight. Now he is gone, and England prays that his sons will be as noble as he was, and will be worthy of their father, Albert the Good. The Queen (Queen Victoria whose beloved husband, Prince-Consort Albert, died in 1861) must reign alone, in splendor and in solitude, for he is gone, but she is royal and will endure. In his closing lines to the Queen, the poet writes:

> ...May all love,
> His love, unseen but felt, o'ershadow thee,
> The love of all thy sons encompass thee,
> The love of all thy daughters cherish thee,
> The love of all thy people comfort thee,
> Till God's love set thee at his side again!

THE COMING OF ARTHUR

Leodogran, the King of Cameliard, had only one daughter, Guinevere. She was the most beautiful of all women and he loved her dearly. This was in the time before Arthur came, when many petty kings and feudal lords ruled in England, and the country was torn asunder by their disputes and wars. In addition, England was frequently subjected to raids by pagan barbarians from the north, who came in ships and laid waste vast areas. Many sections of the country became a wilderness again, and beasts were more at home in them than men. Two kings, Aurelius and Uther, had attempted to reunite the kingdom, but their efforts were unsuccessful. After them, however, Arthur was able for a while to make a nation of England and to rule it through the strength of his Round Table.

At the time the tale begins Cameliard is a deserted wasteland. Leodogran is not strong enough to deal with the situation and often wishes helplessly that the Roman legions would return to restore order. He is attacked nearly simultaneously by Urien, a neighboring king, and a heathen raiding party. Both attackers leave fire and destruction in their wake.

Meanwhile, Arthur has been crowned, despite the protests of those who claim he is not rightful heir to the throne. Leodogran immediately sends to the new King for help. Arthur responds at once to this request and starts his first campaign. At Cameliard he sees Guinevere and instantly falls in love with her. Continuing on his way to the battle, Arthur muses about his love for Guinevere, and decides that with her at his side he will be able to do great things and to be a good King. He plans to ask for her hand in marriage.

In the battle which follows, Arthur and his knights defeat a coalition of enemy kings, including Urien, Carados, Lot of Orkney, and several others. Arthur is pleased at his victory, and especially at the prowess shown by the knight whom he loves most, Lancelot. The two warriors swear an oath of eternal loyalty to each other; Lancelot says:

> "Sir and my liege," he cried, "the fire of God
> Descends upon thee in the battle-field.
> I know thee for my King!"

Arthur answers:

> ..."Man's word is God in man;
> Let chance what will, I trust thee to the death."

After the battle Arthur sends three knights as messengers to Leodogran to ask for Guinevere in marriage. Her father is pleased by the offer, but is uncertain about what to do since he knows the rumors that Arthur is not of royal blood. He questions his faithful chamberlain, but gains no information from him.

Then Leodogran inquires about Arthur's background from the messengers. Bedivere, one of the knights, explains the tale of the King's birth. Many years before in the time of Uther Pendragon, he says, Gorlois of Tintagil wed Ygerne. They had several daughters, among whom is Bellicent, the present queen of Orkney. In a war that followed, Gorlois was killed by Uther and Tintagil Castle was captured. Uther, who had always lusted after Ygerne, forced her to marry him. Their son was Arthur. Uther died before the baby was born; so the child was secretly placed in the care of Merlin, in order to protect him from harm by rivals to the throne. He was raised by an old friend of Uther, Sir Anton, who had purposely acted as if Arthur were one of his own children. This is the basis for the rumors that Arthur was really the son of Anton or Gorlois, and not of Uther. But despite these whispered scandals, Merlin was able to have Arthur crowned when he came of age.

This story notwithstanding, Leodogran is still uncertain about Arthur's parentage and his legal right to the throne, and he doubts also Arthur's ability to hold on to his kingdom. Just at this time, Bellicent of Orkney and her sons, Gawain and Modred, visit at Cameliard. The king questions her too, and she informs him of Arthur's exemplary character and great strength, but she has no precise knowledge about his birth. Leodogran is still unable to make up his mind, but he has a dream which convinces him. He sends the messengers back to Arthur with his acceptance.

Upon learning the news, Arthur dispatches Lancelot and a party of knights to escort Guinevere to him. When she arrives, in May, they are married by Dubric, the head of all the Church in Britain. A great banquet and happy celebrations follow the ceremony, and all of Arthur's followers are overjoyed at his good fortune.

Later on, Arthur refuses to pay the tribute demanded by envoys from Rome, and in twelve great battles he overcomes the heathen and firmly establishes his kingdom.

GARETH AND LYNETTE

Gareth is the youngest son of Lot and Bellicent. His older brothers, Gawain and Modred, have become knights of King Arthur, but he is forced to remain at home with his mother since he is still considered a mere boy. Because of this he is unhappy. He realizes that his mother loves him and that he must be obedient to her wishes, but he is frustrated because a life of chivalry is what he really aspires to.

Finally Gareth speaks to his mother about his desire and, despite her fears, is able to coax her into giving him permission to go to Camelot. She makes only one demand: he must go to Arthur's court in disguise and work for a year as a common kitchen-knave before revealing his identity. She hopes that this demeaning condition will make Gareth reconsider. He remains determined, however; so Bellicent keeps her word and lets him go.

Gareth disguises himself and, accompanied by two servants,

sets out for the magical and rich city of Camelot. They are frightened and awed by the imposing spectacle of the capitol, especially by its high walls on which are sculptures of the Lady of the Lake, symbolizing the True Religion, and the Three Queens, representing Faith, Hope, and Charity. These signify to the whole world the principles by which Arthur guides his Kingdom. Gareth and his servants enter the city and are greeted by Merlin. After a short conversation, he directs them to the palace.

In the great hall Gareth observes the fairness with which Arthur delivers judgments and satisfies the petitions of suppliants. When his turn comes, Gareth asks for and is granted a position as a menial in the palace kitchen. He promises that in a year he will identify himself and fight faithfully for the King.

As time passes, Gareth continues to work in the kitchen. He is popular among the other servants, but is often bullied by his supervisor, Sir Kay. Eventually Gareth learns that Bellicent has relented in her demand and has released him from his one year vow.

Still hiding his name, Gareth begs of the King the right to go on the next quest for which a knight is required. Despite protests from Kay, Arthur grants this request, and permits the boy to keep his identity secret for the time being.

That same day a beautiful and high-born maiden named Lynette appears at the court. She relates a sad story about how her sister Lyonors and the rest of her family are kept prisoners in Castle Perilous by four fierce knights. She has come to Camelot to gain the assistance of the greatest knight, Sir Lancelot, in freeing them. The King agrees to help, but assigns the task to Gareth. Lynette is indignant, for she thinks that Gareth is a lowly kitchen-knave and that this is Arthur's way of insulting her. Nevertheless, Arthur provides Gareth with horse and armor and sends him on the quest.

During the journey to Castle Perilous, Lynette is sullen and unfriendly to Gareth. She frequently berates him for his low birth and lack of ability, and makes him ride several paces behind her. During all this, Gareth remains humble and patient.

While passing through a forest, Gareth rescues a local baron who had been captured by some ruffians, but Lynette declines to credit him for this and attributes his victory to luck. The baron entertains them at his castle. At dinner Lynette refuses to sit at the same table with Gareth. Afterwards, they continue their journey as before.

Eventually the pair arrive at Castle Perilous. One after the other, in hard fights, Gareth vanquishes the first three knights. Very slowly a change begins to come over Lynette's feelings. Initially she only starts to respect his skill and prowess as a warrior, but soon she comes to realize that he is actually of noble birth and, moreover, a chivalrous and honorable knight. She apologizes to him for her previous crude behavior.

Lynette and Gareth are now joined by Lancelot, whom Arthur had sent to protect and assist them. Lancelot's shield is covered when he first approaches, and they do not recognize him. He and Gareth fight and, of course, the youth is defeated. Gareth is mortified and Lynette reproaches him for losing, but Lancelot graciously convinces them that there is no shame in defeat. He offers to fight the fourth knight, since this is what Arthur sent him for, but Gareth refuses. Instead, Lancelot advises Gareth as much as possible in the art of personal combat. Gareth engages the last and most fierce of the knights in a bitter fight and is triumphant. Castle Perilous and the Lady Lyonors are liberated and a merry celebration follows. Later on Gareth and Lynette are wed.

NOTE:
Although one may read it as a purely romantic, adventure tale, this *Idyll* (like several of the others) may be taken also to be a profound allegory. The serpentine river surrounding Castle Perilous can be interpreted as the stream of time. Its three long loops represent the three stages of life — youth, middle-age, and old age — and the three knights at the crossings are the personifications of the temptations typical of these ages, all of which Gareth must overcome in his efforts to be a true knight and worthy of Lynette. The last knight represents Death. The allegorical principle here is that Death, which seems the most formidable of all opponents, is easily defeated, and its defeat yields a new and innocent life.

THE MARRIAGE OF GERAINT

Geraint, tributary prince of Devon and one of Arthur's bravest knights, is married to Enid, the only daughter of Yniol. He loves his wife deeply and she responds with equal affection; her only wish is to please him. The Queen also loves Enid, and is always kind and affectionate to her. In turn, Enid regards Guinevere as the best and most lovely of women. The two ladies are exceptionally good friends.

At this time the first rumors about Lancelot and Guinevere begin to spread through the court, but as yet there is no proof that any romance really exists. Geraint believes the stories and begins to fear that Enid will follow the bad example of her friend, the Queen. His worries begin to plague him and he finally asks Arthur's permission to return to Devon. He pretends that his presence is required in order to rule his province better, but his real reason is to take Enid out from under the suspected evil influence of Guinevere.

The King grants Geraint's request and the couple returns to Devon. After they arrive home, Geraint is very affectionate and attentive to his wife. He totally neglects his duties as a ruler and a knight, for he is obsessed with the idea that Enid has left a lover behind at the palace. Made suspicious by his jealousy, he stays at Enid's side at all times:

Forgetful of his promise to the King,
Forgetful of the falcon and the hunt,
Forgetful of the tilt and tournament,
Forgetful of his glory and his name,
Forgetful of his princedom and its cares.

Before long Geraint's reputation begins to suffer. His people secretly scoff at him and jeer that his manliness is gone. Enid also is upset by his new and disgraceful way of life, but she is afraid to criticize him since she does not want to cause him any pain.

One morning as they lie in bed, she muses out loud about her sad dilemma and berates herself as a bad wife for remaining silent.

Geraint awakens and overhears her last few words. He jumps to the conclusion that she is confessing her infidelity and is infuriated. He angrily shouts that he is still a warrior, despite all rumors, and that he will at once go on a quest in order to prove this. She alone is to accompany him, taking no baggage and wearing her oldest and most shabby dress. Enid asks him the cause of his anger, saying: "If Enid errs, let Enid learn her fault." But Geraint snaps back: "I charge thee, ask not, but obey." Enid does as she is told, recalling as she dresses the last time she had worn these shabby robes.

Many months before on Whitsuntide, Arthur had held his court at Caerleon upon Usk. One day all the court had gone hunting, but Guinevere slept late, dreaming of Lancelot. As she and her servants rode alone to join the others, they met Geraint, who was also late, and had gone on together.

Suddenly they encountered a knight, a lady, and a dwarf riding slowly across their path. When Guinevere's maid inquired who they were, the dwarf struck her, and Geraint received the same treatment when he asked the knight's name. After this odd behavior the three riders continued on their way.

Geraint promised the Queen that he would follow these strangers, in order to learn their names and avenge this insult to Guinevere's majesty. He would return to the court within three days. Since he was unarmed, he planned to provide himself with weapons somewhere along the way. Guinevere wished him good fortune and expressed the hope that he would meet his bride on this quest. If he did, she promised, no matter who the maiden was, Guinevere would herself dress the girl for her wedding and make her a friend.

After following the strangers for a while, Geraint came upon a town in a valley. On one side of the town was a large and new fortress into which the strangers rode, and on the other was an old, run-down castle. Geraint found that all the town's inns were full and that everyone was busy, preparing for a tournament. He learned also that the proud knight was known as the "sparrow-hawk" and that he could get arms and a place to sleep at the old castle.

At the castle Geraint met an aged earl, Yniol, his wife, and Enid, their charming and beautiful daughter. They had no servants and were very poor, but they received him kindly and entertained him as best they could.

As his acquaintance with the family developed, Geraint began to fall in love with Enid, and she with him. After a while he explained his mission in the town. Yniol informed him that the strange knight was his nephew, and had robbed him of his earldom and all his wealth. The noble family, however, bore him no real bitterness. Each year, Yniol continued, the scornful and proud "sparrow-hawk" held a tournament. No knight was permitted to enter unless his lady-love were present, and each year the "sparrow-hawk" won the trophy for his paramour.

Geraint borrowed Yniol's rusty old armor and told the family that he would enter the tournament. Enid was to be his lady-love, and if he won he would marry her. The family was delighted, for they knew Geraint's reputation, and Enid was overjoyed to know that her love was answered.

At the tournament Geraint was victorious and Enid was awarded the prize for beauty. The "sparrow-hawk" admitted his real name to Geraint, and agreed to ride to Caerleon in order to apologize to Guinevere and return the earldom to Yniol. As it happened, Guinevere was kind to the repentant Edyrn, son of Nudd and graciously accepted his apology. Being still young, he completely reformed his character and became a true knight. Edyrn eventually died fighting loyally for Arthur in his last battle.

On the third day Geraint and Enid prepared to return to Caerleon. Remembering the Queen's promise, Geraint asked Enid to wear her oldest dress. The maiden was upset by this, for she feared that her appearence would discredit him at the court. Geraint explained his reason to Enid's mother, and finally Enid complied with her lover's wish.

At Caerleon, Guinevere gladly kept her word, welcomed Enid as a friend, and did her all honor. The Queen personally dressed her on the day of her wedding.

Although all this had taken place many months before, Enid had kept this same old dress in which she had first met Geraint as a keepsake. This is the robe she now puts on in obedience to his harsh order.

GERAINT AND ENID •

Geraint and Enid set out on their journey that very morning. All their troubles, the poet comments, are due to Geraint's susceptibility to the common human failing of not being able to discern between truth and falsity.

Geraint orders Enid to ride in front of him and not to speak, whatever the provocation. Perhaps, Tennyson hints, this is because he still loves her and is afraid that in some outburst of his brooding jealousy he will harm her. Before they have ridden three paces, Geraint shouts:

> ..."Effeminate as I am,
> I will not fight my way with gilded arms,
> All shall be iron...;"

He tosses away his purse and sends his squire home. The two ride on slowly into the bandit-infested wilderness adjoining Devon. Neither speaks, and both look pale and unhappy. Enid muses sadly:

> ..."If there be such in me,
> I might amend it by the grace of Heaven,
> If he would only speak and tell me of it."

After a while, Enid notices three knights and overhears them planning to attack Geraint. He is riding so listlessly that he inspires no fear in them. She does not wish to disobey his order to her, but is afraid that he might be harmed. Finally she rides back and warns him. Rather than show any gratitude, Geraint criticizes Enid for her disobedience and needles her about his suspicion that she really wants him to be defeated. Geraint engages the knights and is victorious. He piles the armor of the dead knights on their horses, and makes Enid lead them as she rides.

The same episode is repeated again with three other knights, and once more Geraint chastises Enid for her disobedience. He is triumphant in the fight. Now Enid is forced to lead six captured horses. Geraint has some sympathy for her difficulty handling them, but does not offer to help.

In the afternoon Geraint and Enid dine with some farm-workers and are then guided to an inn for the night. After arranging for accomodations Geraint continues to be sullen and nasty. Later that evening they are visited at the inn by the local ruler, Earl Limours, who, by chance, happens to once have been a suitor of Enid. Limours is a crude drunkard, and Geraint callously allows him to make all sorts of coarse jokes, much to the distress and embarrassment of Enid. Before leaving for the night, Limours informs Enid that he still loves her, and plans the next morning to rescue her from her cruel husband.

When day breaks, Enid warns Geraint of the plot. He, of course, suspects her of having encouraged the earl and is angry. They leave the inn immediately, but are pursued by Limours and his followers. In a running fight Geraint is able to drive them off.

Soon the unhappy couple enters the lawless territory of Earl Doorm the Bull. Suddenly Geraint collapses, for he had been wounded in the battle with Limours' men, but had said nothing. His injury is a serious one, and Enid is powerless to aid him. She sits by his side weeping while he lies unconscious. All the passers-by are afraid to offer any help.

After a while, Doorm and his soldiers ride past, returning from raid. The outlaw earl's curiosity is aroused by the lovely maiden and he questions her. Doorm insists that the wounded knight is dead, but Enid refuses to believe him. Doorm says:

…"Well, if he be not dead,
Why wail ye for him thus? Ye seem a child.

And he be dead, I count you for a fool;
Your wailing will not quicken him; dead or not,
Ye mar a comely face with idiot tears...."

The outlaw chieftain has his soldiers bring Geraint's body and Enid to his stronghold.

In Doorm's hall that night a banquet takes place. His rough soldiers and their lewd women drink heavily and exchange ribald jests. Meanwhile, Enid sits in a corner tending Geraint's body. She refuses to eat or drink, and is obsessed with the thought that he is still alive. Doorm approaches Enid, and after offering her food, drink, and new clothing, tries to force her to become his mistress. Geraint revives and overhears, but pretends to be dead in order to test Enid's fidelity to him. She continues to refuse Doorm's advances and the earl angrily slaps her. Geraint leaps up and stabs the robber chief. The soldiers and women scatter in panic. Geraint apologizes to Enid for his misuse of her, and then the two flee, fearing that Doorm's spearmen will seek revenge.

As they gallop off together on one horse, they meet Edyrn, son of Nudd. He informs them that he is an advance scout for an army led by Arthur to rid this province of thieves and outlaws. He offers to guide them to the King's camp.

At first Enid is afraid of her cousin, but he informs her that she no longer has any grounds for worry. Through the influence of Guinevere and Dubric, and others at the court, he has become a reformed man and is now a knight of the Round Table.

At the camp Geraint reports to Arthur. The King informs him that his original request to return to Devon had been a reminder of the sorry conditions in this area, and had motivated the present punitive expedition. Moreover, Arthur praises the change in the character of Edyrn and expresses pride in the moral influence that his court has had on the young man. Hearing this causes Geraint to become deeply ashamed of his own blameworthy and pointless behavior.

Geraint's wounds are cared for by the King's own surgeon. In their tent that night, Geraint and Enid are reconciled. Meanwhile, Arthur continues his police operations in this lawless territory. New officers and judges are appointed to "guard the justice of the King," and the army destroys all the bandits strongholds.

When Geraint is well again they all return to Caerleon. Guinevere and Enid renew their friendship, and though Geraint is never again so happy about their relationship as he once was, still he no longer suspects his wife of infidelity.

Later on the happy couple returns to Devon. Geraint's chivalrous and commendable behavior as ruler and knight ends all rumors about him. In time children are born to them and the small family lives a happy and long life together. Never again does Geraint doubt the love or loyalty of Enid. Many years later Geraint dies a noble death while fighting for the King in a battle against the northern heathen.

BALIN AND BALAN

Pellam, one of the former allies of Lot of Orkney, refuses to pay his tribute and Arthur orders his treasurer to go and collect it. The old man informs the King that outside Camelot there are two unknown knights lurking near a fountain, who challenge and overthrow all knights who pass by. Arthur orders the treasurer to avoid them, since he is past the age for fighting.

Later on, the King disguises himself and rides out to meet these knights. They announce that their purpose is to discredit the prowess of all members of the Round Table. Arthur accepts their challenge and defeats them both with great ease.

Afterwards, a herald is sent to call the two knights to the court. On their arrival, Arthur asks their names. One of them replies that they are brothers; he is Balin the Savage and the other is Balan. He explains that three years before, in a fit of rage, he had struck one of Arthur's thralls and was exiled for this crime. He has always been subject to fits of melancholy or madness, and these have intensified since then. Often he would have done violence to himself, but for the interference of Balan, who is a better and more worthy man than himself. During these three bitter years he had decided to defeat a large number of the Round Table's knights. He had thought that this would force Arthur to acknowledge that he was a great knight and he would be readmitted to the King's court. He had been accompanied in this venture by his devoted brother Balan. But today, he continues, his boasts were ended by an unidentified knight who unhorsed them both.

Arthur commends Balin for telling the truth and invites them both to rejoin the Round Table. He says:

> "...As children learn, be thou
> Wiser for falling! walk with me, and move
> To music with thine Order and the King...."

A few days later the embassy to Pellam returns, reporting that this king, who had once been an irreligious and dangerous enemy, has now become very devout. He thinks to prosper in the name of religion, as has Arthur. Pellam claims descent from Joseph of Arimathea, maintains all sorts of religious vigils and obligations, and asserts that he has possession of the very spear with which the Romans had pierced the side of Christ.

Pellam claims to have no further interest in worldly matters, and has put his realm into the control of Garlon, his heir. This man has paid the tribute, but only after many complaints and insults. On their return, the embassy discovered a murdered knight in the woods near Pellam's castle. They had thought Garlon to blame, but soon learned that an evil demon who inhabited the woods was really responsible. Arthur asks for a volunteer to hunt the killer. Balan offers his services and rides off on the quest. Before leaving, he embraces his brother affectionately. He advises Balin to control his moods, and not to be so fearful that others seek to harm him.

In Balan's absence, Balin tries his best to improve himself. He makes a serious effort to become a better knight, and to learn the meaning of courtesy and chivalry. Lancelot, the greatest of all knights, becomes his ideal and he seeks to emulate him in every way. He is also very much under the influence of Guinevere, whom he regards highly, and he bears her token on his shield. With this guidance, Balin soon becomes a figure of respect and admiration in the court. His moods still come over him, but he is able to control them, even though the strain is often great.

One day Balin chances to observe a secret rendezvous between Lancelot and Guinevere. He is shocked by this discovery and his new world begins to fall apart. He loses all faith in himself and his new standards when he sees those whom he respects so much in such a compromising situation. His madness comes upon him again and Balin dashes from the palace in an insane fit.

The deranged knight wanders off in the direction taken by his brother. In his rage he nearly kills a forester, and then attempts to find the demon who infests the woods, hoping to vent his fury on the beast and to purge himself of his madness. Riding carelessly and paying no heed to the warnings he receives, Balin is attacked by the demon. Because of his confused state he is unable to defend himself; he breaks his lance and loses his horse. Finally, much distraught, he arrives on foot at the castle of Pellam.

He is welcomed there and entertained by Garlon. Balin speaks highly of the Queen, but Garlon sneers and repeats the worst scandals that besmirch her reputation. Balin nearly attacks his host in anger, but is just able to restrain himself, and instead tries to deny the gossip.

Nonetheless, Garlon's remarks have upset Balin and trouble him deeply. The next day Garlon taunts him again. Balin attacks him, but shatters his sword in his rage. Garlon is rescued by his soldiers and Balin takes refuge in the chapel where he finds the sacred lance. Using this weapon, he fights his way out of the castle. For many miles he stumbles aimlessly through the woods, until he evades his pursuers. He finds his horse again, and ashamed to have defiled the Queen's token, he throws his shield away. Then Balin bemoans his inability to cope with his madness until he falls into an exhausted sleep.

As Balin lies there, Vivien and her squire ride by on their way to Arthur's court. She is a devotee of the old pagan religion and an enemy of Arthur and his new moral order. She hopes to be able to undermine his power when she arrives at the palace. She sings one of the ancient sun hymns and comments to her squire:

> ..."This fire of heaven,
> This old sun-worship, boy, will rise again,
> And beat the Cross to earth, and break the King
> And all his Table."

When Balin awakens, Vivien asks him to guide her to the court. He refuses, saying that he is no longer worthy to be in the royal presence, and adds that he will stay in the savage woods, where he, another savage, really belongs. He will remain in the forest until his death.

Vivien laughs and Balin thinks she is mocking him. She begs his pardon and tries to convince him that he has no cause for shame, since there is so much vice and corruption at Camelot anyway. She supports her statement by lies and distorted truths. Once again Balin's madness overwhelms him, and cursing himself and them, he dashes deeper into the woods.

Meanwhile, Balan is also in the forest, seeking the demon. He hears Balin's screams and thinks he has found his prey. Snatching his squire's shield he leaps on his horse and rides to the attack. He and Balin fight bitterly, for neither realizes whom the other is.

Vivien and her squire observe these events, and then continue on the way to Camelot. They are both indifferent to what they have seen, and are unable to comprehend the reason for Balin's feelings of shame and guilt.

The two brothers, meanwhile, fatally wound each other. As they lie side by side, they each discover the real identity of their former opponent and realize what a tragic thing has just taken place. Balin moans:

"Oh brother...woe is me!
My madness all thy life has been thy doom,
Thy curse, and darken'd all thy day; and now
The night has come. I scarce can see thee now.
Good night! for we shall never bid again
Good morrow — Dark my doom was here, and dark
It will be there. I see thee now no more.
I would not mine again should darken thine;
Good night, true brother."
                                    Balan answer'd low,
"Good night, true brother, here! good morrow there!
We two were born together, and we die
Together by one doom:" and while he spoke
Closed his death-drowsing eyes, and slept the sleep
With Balin, either lock'd in either's arm.

MERLIN AND VIVIEN

The air is still, but a storm is brewing. Merlin and Vivien are resting beneath an oak tree in the forest of Broceliande.

Much earlier, Arthur's enemy, Mark of Cornwall, had learned the rumors current in Camelot: that Lancelot and the Queen were carrying on an adulterous affair in secret. He was also told that the influence of this corruption was slowly spreading among others at the court. Mark decided to send Vivien, his paramour, to Camelot, in order that she might take advantage of this delicate situation and stir up additional trouble.

Upon her arrival at court, Vivien had appealed to Guinevere for sanctuary and claimed to be an innocent, orphan maiden who had just escaped from the torments of Mark. Her request was granted and Vivien was made one of the ladies in waiting. Having attained this position, Vivien spent her time ferreting out information, spreading scandalous stories, and causing other kinds of unrest. As part of her plan, she attempted to gain the confidence of

Arthur, but the King wanted nothing to do with her. The story of Vivien's failure spread through the court and made her a subject of laughter for a while. This only served to infuriate her and to make her more determined in her evil intentions.

One of the most famous and important men in Camelot was Merlin, the great magician, astronomer, engineer, architect, and bard, whose friendship and wise advice were valuable assets to Arthur. Vivien made a concerted effort to gain the old man's favor. She eventually succeeded, for though he did not like her, he was amused by her feline mannerisms and complimented by her attentions. Vivien even claimed to be in love with him. Merlin was too wise to believe this, but he was old and lonely, and sometimes his certainty would weaken.

A time came when Merlin fell into a state of deep depression. He wandered alone on the beach and then drifted off in a small boat that he found, but Vivien followed and joined him. At first he was unaware of her presence; then he pretended to ignore her. Finally they came ashore in Brittany and continued to wander until they reached the forest of Broceliande. Vivien had gone to all this effort because she recalled that Merlin had once mentioned a potent magic charm he knew. Through this spell a man could be made as if imprisoned in an impregnable tower, and would be invisible to all the world except the one who worked the charm. Vivien now sought to learn this secret and use it on Merlin. This is how the two came to be resting together in the forest.

As they recline beneath the tree, Vivien caresses and kisses Merlin's feet and beard, and chatters to him of her love and devotion. Merlin is delighted by her talk, but does not believe even a part of it. Nonetheless, since he owes her a boon, he promises to grant her wish. Vivien asks to be taught the secret charm, as an expression of his trust in her and proof that he returns her love, but Merlin refuses. In addition, he berates himself for ever having revealed the existence of the secret to her. He justifies his refusal by his fears that she would misuse the charm, and offers her anything else she desires.

Vivien now begins to make use of all her varied feminine devices in order to lure Merlin into her trap; she is coy, she weeps, she sings:

> " 'In love, if love be love, if love be ours,
> Faith and unfaith can ne'er be equal powers:
> Unfaith in aught is want of faith in all.' "

For an instant Merlin nearly believes her to be truly in love with him, but he manages to regain his senses.

He attempts to distract Vivien by telling her anecdotes about his youth, but she always manages to guide the conversation back to the same subject: whether or not he responds equally to her love for him, and whether he will continue to "mistreat" her and "exploit" her devotion. Merlin continues to deny her request. Now Vivien pretends to be indignant, as if he had insulted her. Finally Merlin tells her the ancient legend attached to the origin of the charm, hoping to satisfy her that way. But this indication of lessening resistance encourages Vivien. She maintains her assault on him, and uses every wile to seduce him to her wishes.

As their conversation continues, it is evident that Merlin really understands what a vicious and evil person Vivien is, but he is old and tired, and cannot help but find her pretended affection for him complimentary. In one last effort, he orders her to leave him, and calls her a harlot. Vivien is angered, but she hides her rage and behaves as if she were a wronged and misused maiden. She swears she is innocent of evil intentions, and refuses to respond to any more of his advances. Finally, in terror of the impending storm, she throws herself upon Merlin for protection. His resistance is now at its lowest ebb; he takes pity on her, teaches her the charm, and falls into an exhausted sleep.

> Then, in one moment, she put forth the charm
> Of woven paces and of waving hands,
> And in the hollow oak he lay as dead,
> And lost to life and use and name and fame.

Then crying, "I have made his glory mine,"
And shrieking out, "O fool!" the harlot leapt
Adown the forest, and the thicket closed
Behind her, and the forest echo'd "fool."

LANCELOT AND ELAINE

The fair and loveable Elaine, known as the lily maid of Astolat, sits alone in her chamber high in a tower, where she watches over the shield of Sir Lancelot. She devotes all her energies to protecting this shield from rust or other harm, and has made an elaborately embroidered silk cover for it. She is with the shield so often that she is familiar with every scratch and dent in it, and knows the stories behind them. In her fantasies she relives the thrilling battles and jousts that they recall.

How is it that this innocent maiden has Lancelot's shield, especially when once she did not even know his name? Some time ago the shield was left in her care by its owner when he rode off to take part in a great tournament at which the King was to present a valuable diamond to the winner.

Long before he was crowned, Arthur had come into possession of nine valuable jewels, which he often displayed proudly at his court. Each year he sponsored a tournament at which one of these was presented to the winner. In this, the ninth year, only the largest of the diamonds remained. At each of the previous contests Lancelot had won the prize. He had saved the jewels and secretly planned to offer them as a gift to the Queen, after he had the entire set.

Now it was time again for the tournament, and the court was moving from London to Camelot for the great event. Guinevere had recently recovered from a severe illness and asked permission to remain behind. Upon learning this, Lancelot went to the King and, claiming that one of his old wounds was bothering him again, also obtained leave to stay in London.

After the others had gone, Guinevere began to carp at Lancelot for what he had done, pointing out that he had merely provided additional material for those who delighted in slandering them. Both their reputations would suffer, she said, and for no good reason. Lancelot was annoyed at her reaction, partly from disappointment and partly because he resented having lied in vain. He inquired whether the King had expressed any suspicions about their relationship, and asked sarcastically, whether she was now tired of him and preferred her husband.

Guinevere laughed scornfully and said:

"Arthur, my lord, Arthur, the faultless King,
That passionate perfection, my good lord —
But who can gaze upon the sun in heaven?
He never spake word of reproach to me,
He never had a glimpse of mine untruth,
He cares not for me. Only here to-day
There gleamed a vague suspicion in his eyes;
        ....to me
He is all fault who hath no fault at all.
For who loves me must have a touch of earth;
The low sun makes the color. I am yours,
Not Arthur's, as ye know, save by the bond...."

The Queen suggested that Lancelot go to the tournament after all, in order to avoid harmful gossip. He was worried about the excuse he would make, but she planned that he would participate in the jousts while disguised. Then he could say that the ploy had been planned in advance, so that he could prove that he still retained all his knightly prowess, and was not just thriving on his reputation. Arthur, she predicted, would be delighted by this tale.

Lancelot set out for the tournament, riding alone, and on the way stopped at the castle of Astolat. There he was entertained by the lord of the place, his sons Sir Torre and Sir Lavaine, and his beautiful daughter, Elaine. He did not identify himself, but it was easy enough for them to determine that he was a great knight and from the royal court.

The shy and innocent young Elaine had naturally been attracted to the handsome, noble, and experienced knight. Lancelot made no advances, but because of his chivalrous nature, he was kind and attentive to her. Elaine's naivete made her misunderstand this. She sat enthralled as he told them tales of the King's court and battles, and before long she had fallen in love with him.

The next morning Lancelot borrowed an old shield and left his own in Elaine's care, in order to complete his disguise. She asked him to wear her favor on his helmet, and although he had never honored any woman in this way before, he agreed when she pointed out that it would also add to his disguise.

Lancelot left for Camelot in the company of Sir Lavaine. On the way he told his companion his real identity. Meanwhile, Elaine stayed at Astolat, watching over the shield and daydreaming about the man whom she loved.

At the tournament no one recognized Lancelot and all were surprised at the amazing success of this unknown knight. Lancelot's friends and relatives, however, were angered at this stranger's presumption in trying to outdo their hero's reputation, and attacked him. He was outnumbered and seriously wounded. Despite this, he was still the obvious winner and was invited to accept the prize, but Lancelot cried out:

...."Diamond me
No diamonds! for God's love, a little air!
Prize me no prizes, for my prize is death!"

Bidding them not to follow, Lancelot fled from the field accompanied by Lavaine. The two knights took refuge with a hermit they knew, and attempted to staunch the flow of blood from the wound.

Meanwhile, Arthur assigned Sir Gawain to follow and find the unknown knight, in order to award him the diamond. Much against his will, for he preferred the pleasant life at court, Gawain set out on his mission.

Later on the Queen was told about the events at the tournament. She told Arthur that the mysterious knight had really been Lancelot. When Guinevere learned that Lancelot had worn a lady's favor in his helmet, she was shocked and upset. She tried to hide her distress at this news, but soon became very morose and suffered bitter pangs of jealousy and suspicion.

It is about at this point in the story that Elaine sits in her tower, guarding the shield. On his mission, Gawain eventually comes to Astolat. In conversation with Elaine he learns about the shield and soon identifies it as belonging to Lancelot. Despite Arthur's explicit instructions, Gawain leaves the jewel with Elaine, reasoning that Lancelot must, after all, come back for his shield. He eagerly returns to Camelot where he is chided by the King for not fully carrying out his orders. At the same time, though, Gawain derives much malicious pleasure from spreading tales about the love of Lancelot for Elaine. Guinevere is hurt by all this new gossip from jealousy, but also from what she considers an insulting blow to her pride.

Ever since she learned about Lancelot's wound from Gawain, Elaine has been very worried about him. Accompanied by her older brother, she sets out to find him. They finally discover Lancelot with Lavaine, in a hermit's cell close to Camelot. The wound has become infected and he is lying near death.

With much effort and patience, Elaine is able to nurse Lancelot back to health. All through his illness, she dreams and hopes that he also loves her. When he is well, they all return to Astolat for the shield, and it is here that Lancelot first learns of Elaine's love for him. He is deeply moved, and admits that he regards her as a dear friend or sister, but states that it is impossible for him to marry her. He has no desire to cause her pain, and is as gentle as the circumstances allow, but despite his considerate attitude, Elaine is heartbroken. Lancelot returns to Camelot, and after he goes she becomes seriously ill. She refuses to eat and loses all will to live.

Within a few days she dies, after having left certain strict instructions to her bereaved family.

Several days later Lancelot is finally granted a private audience by Guinevere. He presents her with his gift, but the Queen coldly accuses him of infidelity to her. In her anger she tosses the diamonds from her window into the river below. Lancelot looks out, and he sees a barge draped in black floating on the water, bearing the body of a young maiden.

Lancelot hastens to the landing place, where many other members of the court, including the King, have also gathered. Everyone is awed by the mysterious spectacle before them. Two knights bear the body into the palace, and Arthur reads aloud the letter that was clutched in her dead hand. It says:

"Most noble lord, Sir Lancelot of the Lake,
I, sometime call'd the maid of Astolat,
Come, for you left me taking no farewell,
Hither, to take my last farewell of you.
I loved you and my love had no return,
And therefore my true love has been my death.
And therefore to our Lady Guinevere,
And to all other ladies, I make moan:
Pray for my soul, and yield me burial.
Pray for my soul thou too, Sir Lancelot,
As thou art a knight peerless."

Everyone is affected by this touching letter. Lancelot tells the whole sad story to Arthur and the assembled courtiers. He also arranges for Elaine's burial.

Later Arthur comments to Lancelot that it is a pity he did not wed such a lovely maiden, since he is so lonely. It is true that Lancelot is unhappy, but he is unable to make an answer to this remark. The Queen quietly forgives him and apologizes for her suspicions, but somehow Lancelot is still not satisfied. He wanders alone, meditating about his life and the sins he has committed, and about his infidelity to his dearest friend, Arthur. And so, he suffers intense remorse and pain.

THE HOLY GRAIL

After a full life as a knight, Sir Percivale retires to an abbey near Camelot, and there becomes a monk. Shortly afterwards, he dies. Ambrosius, one of the other monks, had become his friend, and during the last days of his life, Percivale told his companion about the vision of the Holy Grail which had changed his life, and finally caused him to leave the Round Table for a life of austerity and prayer.

The tale is as follows:

Following the death of Christ, Joseph of Arimathea had wandered through the world until he came to Glastonbury, where he settled and built the first Christian Church in England. With him he had brought the Grail, the very cup which Christ had used at His last supper. The cup had remained as a holy relic at the church, and often the mere touching of it had healed the sick. Finally the evil of the times became so great that the cup had disappeared from earth and returned to heaven.

Percivale had a sister, a very holy and devout maiden, who was a nun. The corruption and sin that was beginning to appear at Arthur's court greatly disturbed her, and she often fasted and prayed for salvation. Her confessor had told her the story of the Grail and explained that when men were pure again it would return to earth. When the Round Table was founded, it was expected that the Grail would reappear, but sin soon began to decay even that institution. Despite all their hopes, the faithful continued to be disappointed. The nun continued to pray and fast, trusting that she would be blessed with a personal vision of the Grail. One day she called Percivale to her and told him that this had indeed come to pass.

Percivale spread this news among his fellow knights, all of whom became excited by this new prospect for salvation. Many of them, including himself, and Galahad, who was renowned as the purest of men, began to keep strict religious vigils. Then one day a miracle took place.

There was a vacant chair at the Round Table, made by Merlin before he had disappeared, and known as the "Siege Perilous." There was an inscription on it which warned that "there no man could sit but he should lose himself." Galahad read this and said: "If I lose myself, I save myself!" and sat in the chair.

There was a sudden crash of thunder and a beam of bright light; the Grail appeared before the assembled knights, and veiled in a cloud, moved slowly past them. Everyone saw his companion as if in the midst of divine glory, and all were inspired by the experience. The knights were silent until Percivale said:

"I sware a vow...that I,
Because I had not seen the Grail, would ride
A twelvemonth and a day in quest of it,
Until I found and saw it, as the nun
My sister saw it..."

The same oath was taken by Galahad, Bors, Lancelot, Gawain, and most of the other knights.

Now on this day, the King along with a number of his knights had been on a campaign against a band of robbers, and so had not been present when all this occurred. Now they returned to Camelot and entered the hall, bloody and dirty from their battle. They found the place in a tumult of confusion, but rapidly learned what had happened. The King was distressed at the news:

...'Woe is me, my knights,' he cried,
'Had I been here, ye had not sworn the vow.'

He questioned man after man, and discovered that none except Galahad had actually seen the Grail. Furthermore, Galahad had also heard a voice calling upon him to follow.

' "Ah, Galahad, Galahad,' said the King, 'for such
As thou art is the vision, not for these...' "

Arthur continued to explain that Galahad and the nun were both holy, chaste individuals, and were worthy of the vision. For the others to attempt to attain that of which they were not worthy was foolhardy and presumptuous. As knights they were required to adhere to their vows, but in their absence, he feared, much evil would be allowed to spread unchecked through the realm, and much of their work would be undone. Many of them, he said, would never return, and the Round Table, and all it stood for, would be destroyed.

The next day a great tournament was held, for Arthur wanted to see all his knights assembled together for one last time. Afterwards, those who had taken the vow set out on their quests. As they rode through the gates of Camelot, the people wept or watched sadly. The King was barely able to speak, and Guinevere cried out: "This madness has come on us for our sins."

When he left the city, Percivale continued, he felt morally uplifted and confident. Thereafter, though, he learned that Arthur's forbodings had been justified, for he wandered aimlessly through the countryside and a deep depression came over him. The memory of his past evil thoughts and deeds cried out: "This quest is not for thee."

As Percivale searched he was beset by doubts and by many temptations. Nothing satisfied the deep craving within his soul, however, and he had a continual feeling of frustration and aimlessness. During his wandering, he slowly learned that the things he valued most were illusions, and, not knowing what to do, he became more melancholy.

Finally Percivale met a simple hermit, to whom he told his story. The holy man responded:

" 'Oh son, thou hast not true humility,
The highest virtue, mother of them all....
Thou hast not lost thyself to save thyself
As Galahad.' "

At that moment, Galahad himself appeared in the little chapel. He was dressed in silver armor, and had a mystical quality about him.

The three men prayed together. During their devotions Percivale saw nothing, but Galahad had another vision of the Grail. It was bloody red in color, and was seen in the midst of flames. This vision had been with him since he left Camelot. In that time he had roamed through the world, smashing the pagan hordes and ending their evil customs. Now, he knew, his time was at hand and he would be received into the heavenly city. He invited Percivale to accompany him part of the way, for then he too would be able to see the vision. Overwhelmed by the force of Galahad's faith, Percivale agreed.

The two knights climbed to the top of a nearby high hill, and then walked to the edge of the sea. Percivale watched as Galahad entered a boat and drifted away. He saw, over the chaste knight's head, the Grail itself, glowing in the air. He had also a vision of the spiritual city into which Galahad entered. Then everything vanished. Percivale knew that he had at last seen the Grail and that it would never again return to earth. He was satisfied, and the next day he went back to Camelot.

On his way, Percivale met Sir Bors, and learned of this knight's brief vision of the Grail. Bors also told him of the madness which had afflicted Lancelot, as a result of the conflict between his desire to see the vision and his guilt for his sins.

At Camelot Percivale and Bors discovered a scene of tragic desolation and ruin. Only a tiny fraction of his knights still remained with Arthur, for many had died or disappeared. The survivors were haggard and worn. The King himself was very morose. Gawain and the others had finally admitted that they were not worthy of the vision, but the harm done by their quest was irreparable. Even Lancelot had returned, and reported that after many adventures he had seen a vision in which the Grail had appeared, but not with sufficient clarity for him to make it out. He upbraided himself severely for his unworthiness.

Arthur and the knights discussed the events that had taken place, and the King solemnly said:

" '...if indeed there came a sign from heaven,
Blessed are Bors, Lancelot, and Percivale,

For these have seen according to their sight....
And spake I not truly, O my knights?
Was I too dark a prophet when I said
To those who went upon the Holy Quest,
That most of them would follow wandering fires,
Lost in the quagmire?—lost to me and gone....
And some among you held that if the King
Had seen the sight he would have sworn the vow.
Not easily, seeing that the King must guard
That which he rules...
(And) may not wander...
Before his work be done...
And knows himself no vision to himself,
Nor the high God a vision, nor that One
Who rose again. Ye have seen what ye have seen.'"

And ending his tale, Percivale said:

"So spake the King; I knew not all he meant."

PELLEAS AND ETTARRE

In order to fill the gaps left in the ranks of the Round Table after the quest for the Grail, Arthur begins to appoint a number of new knights. While the court is in Caerleon, a handsome and idealistic youth named Pelleas approaches the King and says:

"Make me thy knight, because I know, Sir King,
All that belongs to knighthood, and I love."

The lad is particularly eager to enter the forthcoming tournament. Pelleas provides Arthur with excellent references and is made a knight.

One day Sir Pelleas of the Isles, as he is now known, is riding to Camelot. It is the height of midsummer and the heat makes him delirious. He rests beneath a shady tree and dreams of the maiden whom he will someday love, whispering to himself:

...."Where?

O, where? I love thee, tho' I know thee not.
For fair thou art and pure as Guinevere,
And I will make thee with my spear and sword
As famous — O my Queen, my Guinevere,
For I will be thine Arthur when we meet."

Pelleas continues on his way and suddenly encounters a party of ladies and knights. They are lost and ask him the way to the city. Pelleas gazes at the woman who is the leader of the group and is overwhelmed by her beauty and poise. He is embarrassed and can only stammer an answer to her questions, for he grew up in an isolated area where the only women were those of his family and household.

The lady, Ettarre, is cold and scornful when she sees his shyness, but Pelleas finally agrees to guide her party to the city. Ettarre mutters to herself about the ignorance of this callow youth. She sees also that he is a gallant knight, and decides to take advantage of his affection for her. She plans to make him win the tournament and present the trophy to her.

Ettarre and her friends are kind to the youth. At Camelot she takes his hand in hers and says:

                    ..."Oh the strong hand...
See! Look at mine! but wilt thou fight for me,
And win me this fine circlet, Pelleas,
That I may love thee?"

The inexperienced youth is completely fooled by her pretence and is overjoyed to think that his love for Ettarre is answered. He resolves to win the tourney so that she will be proud of him.

A few days later "The Tournament of Youth" is held. Because of his love for Pelleas, Arthur restrains his veteran knights from entering, and the youth wins an honorable victory. He presents the prize to Ettarre, and this is the last time that she ever behaves decently to him.

For the remainder of her stay at court, the wicked Ettarre ignores Pelleas. When she returns home, Pelleas hopefully follows her party. Obeying Ettarre's orders, her maidens and knights mock and abuse Pelleas throughout the journey. At the end of the trip they lock Pelleas out of her castle.

The boy is confused by these events and sadly reassures himself:

"These be the ways of ladies...
To those who love them, trials of our faith.
Yea, let her prove me to the uttermost,
For loyal to the uttermost am I."

For the next few days Pelleas waits outside the castle for Ettarre to call him. She becomes indignant and annoyed at his constant presence beneath the walls. She sends her knights to chase him away, but he defeats each of them.

Another day her knights assault him all at once, bind him, and bring him inside. Pelleas pleads his love for Ettarre, but the callous woman curses him bitterly and orders him to leave her alone. Then she has him released.

Nevertheless, a week later Pelleas is still outside. Ettarre sends her knights again, with orders to capture or kill him. At this moment Sir Gawain passes by. He is enraged by this unfair fight and attempts to aid Pelleas. The youth asks him not to join in, however, and allows himself to be captured.

In the castle Pelleas is reproached and mistreated by Ettarre, although she muses quietly to herself at his love for her. She has her knights eject him from the castle.

Outside Gawain unties Pelleas and listens to his story. He too is scornful about Pelleas' behavior and lectures him sternly about the code of honor of the Round Table. Then he offers to go to Ettarre and set things right for the youth. He asks Pelleas to return to the castle in three days.

During this time, Pelleas wanders aimlessly in the surrounding country, confused and beset by doubts. On the third day he returns but Gawain does not meet him. The youth sneaks into the castle, and to his great dismay discovers Gawain and Ettarre sleeping side by side. He is tempted to kill them both, but remembering his oath of chivalry he is unable to commit murder. He leaves his sword between the two bodies and gallops off in a fury.

As he rides, Pelleas moans to himself about what a fool he has been. He feels that he is totally disgraced and dishonored, and is especially upset because he was unable to revenge himself on Gawain and Ettarre. He blames all his troubles on Arthur, rationalizing that if the King had not taught him a noble moral code, he would not be so troubled by its violation.

Pelleas rides without direction, and is made half-mad by his unhappy memories and thoughts. Weary and thirsty, he encounters Percivale, who is now a monk. Percivale tends the sick youth, and overhears him cry out in his sleep: "False! and I held thee pure as Guinevere." Later on, Percivale makes a sarcastic remark about Guinevere's purity. He is horrified to discover that the lad has no knowledge of Guinevere's real nature. Pelleas asks:

"Is the Queen false?" and Percivale was mute.
"Have any of our Round Table held their vows?"
And Percivale made answer not a word.
"Is the King true?" "The King!" said Percivale.
"Why, then let men couple at once with wolves.
What! art thou mad?"

Pelleas leaps up again and rides away, nearly killing his horse in his fury. He is slowly being driven insane by the collapse of the illusions he has held about himself and the Round Table. He continues riding until he reaches Camelot, which he calls a "black nest of rats."

Outside the city, Pelleas sees Lancelot. In a frenzy, the youth attacks the knight. Lancelot refuses to fight, but the boy shouts insanely that he is an avenger come to punish the sins of the Round

Table. Lancelot is forced to overthrow the youth in self-defense. Pelleas asks to be slain, but the knight refuses, and sadly leads him back to the city.

At the court Pelleas sees all the knights and ladies, among whom is Guinevere. The Queen hears Lancelot's story and says to the boy:

> ..."O young knight,
> Hath the great heart of knighthood in thee fail'd
> So far thou canst not bide, unfrowardly,
> A fall from *him*?" Then, for he answer'd not,
> "Or hast thou other griefs? If I, the Queen,
> May help them, loose thy tongue, and let me know."
> But Pelleas lifted up an eye so fierce
> She quail'd; and he, hissing "I have no sword,"
> Sprang from the door into the dark. The Queen
> Look'd hard upon her lover, he on her,
> And each foresaw the dolorous day to be;
> And all talk died, as in a grove all song
> Beneath the shadow of some bird of prey.
> Then a long silence came upon the hall,
> And Modred thought, "The time is hard at hand."

THE LAST TOURNAMENT

Little Dagonet, King Arthur's fool, dances gaily about the hall. Towards him, carrying a harp and a jeweled trophy won in yesterday's tournament, walks Sir Tristram, saying: "Why skip ye so, Sir Fool?"

Some while before, Arthur and Lancelot had found an abandoned child wearing this jeweled crown in a desolate wilderness. They had brought the infant back to Camelot to be reared by the Queen. Guinevere soon came to love the baby very much, but the the child took sick and died. In her distress, the Queen suggested that a tournament be held and the infant's crown be given as the prize. She said: "Who knows?—the purest of thy knights may win ...for the purest of my maids."

On the morning of this tournament, one of Arthur's servants staggered into the hall. He reported that he had been beaten and wounded by the Red Knight and his followers. He had been given a message for the King from the Red Knight, as follows:

" 'Tell thou the King and all his liars that I
Have founded my Round Table in the North,
And whatsoever his own knights have sworn
My knights have sworn the counter to it—and say
My tower is full of harlots, like his court…and say
My knights are all adulterers like his own,
But mine are truer, seeing they profess
To be none other; and say his hour is come,
The heathen are upon him, his long lance
Broken, and his Excalibur a straw.' "

Arthur immediately announced that he, accompanied only by his youngest knights, would ride north to rid the region of renegades and outlaws. In his absence, he ordered, the tournament was to be held anyway, and Lancelot was to preside.

The next day "The Tournament of the Dead Innocence" took place. Some related this name only to the unexpected death of the infant, but others saw a deeper and more serious symbolism in it.

At this tournament the corruption and decay that had been brewing in Camelot came to the surface. All the rules of chivalry and fairness were broken by the participants. There was cheating of every kind. Lancelot and the umpires observed all the violations, but they did not dare protest. The winner of the day was Sir Tristram.

While making the award, Lancelot caustically inquired whether Tristram was really the purest of Arthur's knights, for the man was well known to be an adulterer. Tristram responded bitterly, and made several sarcastic comments about Lancelot and Guinevere. These remarks, in addition to his statements about the low standards of morality prevalent in Camelot shocked many in the audience. They muttered: "All courtesy is dead…the glory of our Round Table is no more."

A banquet was planned for the next day, and it is at this dinner that Tristram and Dagonet meet. The two men hold a long conversation in which, despite his fool's costume and manner, Dagonet appears as a perceptive observer of affairs at court. Tristram, on the other hand, seems to be the real fool. Dagonet's statements show him to be one of the few left in Camelot who retains faith in Arthur and his principles.

Afterwards, Tristram rides to Lyonnesse to seek Isolt, his lover. Both he and she are married to others, but they will not let this detail interfere with their romance.

Meanwhile, in the north, Arthur and his small army are on campaign. The King wins a bloody victory:

So all the ways were safe from shore to shore,
But in the heart of Arthur pain was lord.

He is beginning to perceive the decay of the institutions he has founded and the ideals he has upheld. In addition, he has a premonition of his own downfall.

Tristram arrives at Tintagil where Isolt lives with her husband, King Mark. He surprises her in her chamber. At first she is jealous, having learned of his marriage, but he is soon able to allay her suspicions. She tells Tristram of her own hatred for her cruel husband. The two lovers sit and talk together for several hours, recalling memories of their past happiness. The poet subtly relates the development of their love and the vows they have broken, to the general moral breakdown of the Round Table. Tristram presents Isolot with her gift, and is about to kiss her when Mark breaks into the room and stabs him in the back.

That same night Arthur returns to Camelot and finds the palace dark and silent. The Queen's room is vacant and gloom is everywhere. Only Dagonet is present. The jester falls at the King's feet and sobs:

...."I am thy fool,
And I shall never make thee smile again."

GUINEVERE

Arthur's nephew, the villainous Modred, has been planning for a long time to usurp the throne. He is assisted in his evil designs by Vivien. Together they take advantage of every opportunity to arouse discord and treason at the court.

One night, while the King is away, Modred is able to trap Lancelot and the Queen in her chamber. In the confusion which follows, several of Modred's followers are slain, Lancelot flees to his feudal domain in France, and Guinevere takes refuge in the abbey at Almesbury. Here she is given sanctuary by the nuns, even though they are not aware of her real identity.

For the next few weeks, Guinevere lives at the abbey, suffers from a serious depression, and speaks with no one except the young novice who serves as her maid. One night they receive startling news: Arthur, who believed Lancelot a traitor, had been waging war on him in France. Meanwhile he left Modred as regent in his place. After having formed an alliance with the northern heathen and various unfaithful lords, Arthur's wicked nephew has made himself King. Arthur is now returning to England with his army.

When Guinevere learns this, and realizes that the awful state of the kingdom is in large part due to her own behavior, she moans: "With what a hate the people and King must hate me."

The young novice attempts to cheer the weeping lady, but has little success. In order to distract her, the nun repeats all the old stories and prophecies about Arthur, the great achievements of his reign, and the eventual decay of his Round Table. She attributes the moral downfall to the sin first committed by the Queen and Lancelot. Upon hearing this, Guinevere's grief becomes more intense. She orders the nun to leave her chamber.

Alone, Guinevere muses about herself and remembers some happy episodes of her life with Arthur. Her thoughts ramble on and she indulges in self-pity. Suddenly an armed knight rides into the courtyard, and a whisper runs through the abbey: "The King! The King!" A few seconds more and Arthur confronts Guinevere in her room.

The King's demeanor is saddened, for he has at last learned the truth about Guinevere's infidelity, and now he forsees his own impending defeat and death. He is, however, a majestic figure as he stands before her. Arthur speaks to his wife at great length, saying in part:

..."I did not come to curse thee, Guinevere....
Lo, I forgive thee...do thou for thine own soul the rest....
Let no man dream but that I love thee still....
Hereafter in that world where all are pure
We two may meet before high God, and thou
Wilt spring to me, and claim me thine, and know
I am thine husband.... Leave me that,
I charge thee, my last hope. Now must I hence.
...to lead mine hosts
Far down to that great battle in the west,
Where I must strike against the man they call
My sister's son...who leagues
With...heathen, and knights,
Traitors—and strike him dead, and meet myself
Death, or I know not what mysterious doom.
And thou remaining here wilt learn the event;
But hither shall I never come again,
Never lie by thy side, see thee no more—
Farewell!"

After Arthur leaves, Guinevere becomes hysterical for she has learned that she still loves him, and understands at last the full significance and consequence of her immorality.

In the years that follow she remains at the abbey and devotes her life to penance and good works. After a while, in virtue of her good deeds and pure life, she is made abbess. She dies there, beloved by the nuns and all the inhabitants of the surrounding country.

THE PASSING OF ARTHUR

This is the story told by Sir Bedivere, the last survivor of the Round Table.

One night on the march westward, Bedivere overhears Arthur lamenting in his tent. The King is perplexed and confused by recent events, the failure of the institutions he has founded, and the people whom he trusted. He speaks of his belief in God and muses:

"I found Him in the shining of the stars,
I mark'd Him in the flowering of His fields,
But in His ways with men I find Him not.
...for why is all around us here
As if some lesser god had made the world,
But had not force to shape it as he would...."

Arthur finally wonders whether God has forsaken him after all his efforts, and concludes:

"My God, thou hast forgotten me in my death!
Nay—God, my Christ—I pass but shall not die."

Another night the ghost of Gawain, killed in the war with Lancelot, comes to plague Arthur, howling:

...."Hollow, hollow all delight!
Hail, King! to-morrow thou shalt pass away.
Farewell!..."

At this Arthur cries out, and Bedivere tries to comfort him by reminding the King of his past glories. He points out that the rebels still recognize Arthur's sovereignty, and that he should "Arise, go forth and conquer as of old."

Arthur answers that the forthcoming battle is of a different sort from any previous one. In the past they have fought only enemies, but now they must fight his own former subjects, and:

"...The king who fights his people fights himself.
And they my knights, who loved me once, the stroke
That strikes them dead is as my death to me..."

No matter though, Arthur continues, they must go on in whatever path destiny has outlined for them, and attempt to solve each new problem as it arises.

At long last the two armies meet in the wilderness near Lyonnesse. The battle is fought under the most weird and terrifying conditions; the air is cold and still, and a thick white mist covers the entire field so that no one can see his adversary. Blinded by the fog, many warriors kill their own friends or relatives, and others have strange visions of ghosts and past events. The battle is a savage one, and many deeds of great nobility, as well as many of cowardice and evil, take place on the field. Everywhere Arthur fights in the midst of the fierce conflict.

Finally the day comes to an end. Arthur stands with Bedivere, and the two survey the heaps of hacked, bloody corpses. They are the victors, but Arthur sadly points out that he seems King only among the dead. Suddenly they notice that Modred too has survived. Arthur attacks the traitor and kills him, but Modred, as his last act, mortally wounds the King.

Sir Bedivere carries the dying King to a nearby chapel and attempts to tend his wound. Arthur realizes that his end is nigh, and instructs his faithful follower to take his royal sword, Excalibur, and throw it into the lake outside.

The sword is so beautiful that Bedivere feels it should be saved, as a memorial of Arthur and his ideals for later generations. Twice he pretends to have obeyed the command and both times Arthur recognizes that Bedivere is not telling the truth. He insists that the knight carry out this one last order.

Bedivere throws the sword toward the center of the lake, but an arm wrapped in white cloth reaches out to catch it. After brandishing Excalibur in the air three times, the arm draws it into the water. When Arthur hears this, he asks Bedivere to carry him to the edge of the lake.

When they arrive at the shore they see a barge draped in black slowly drawing up to them. On the deck stand three queens, dressed in black and wearing golden crowns. They lift Arthur into the barge, wash his wounds, and weep as they do so.

Bedivere asks Arthur what is to become of him, now that the Round Table is destroyed, and justice has vanished from the world. Arthur answers:

> "The old order changeth, yielding place to new,
> And God fulfils himself in many ways,
> Lest one good custom should corrupt the world.
> Comfort thyself: what comfort is in me?
> I have lived my life, and that which I have done
> May He within himself make pure! but thou,
> If thou shouldst never see my face again,
> Pray for my soul....
> But now farewell. I am going a long way
> With these thou seest...
> To the island-valley of Avilion;
> Where falls not hail, or rain, or any snow,
> Nor ever wind blows loudly; but it lies
> Deep-meadow'd, happy, fair with orchard lawns
> And bowery hollows crown'd with summer sea,
> Where I will heal me of my grievous wound."

With this, the barge sails off and Arthur is never seen again.

Bedivere stands watching for a long time, reliving many memories, until the boat is just a tiny dot on the horizon. He groans to himself: "The King is gone... From the great deep to the great deep he goes." Bedivere slowly turns and walks away, murmuring:

> "He passes to be King among the dead,
> And after healing of his grievous wound
> He comes again...."

In the distance Bedivere hears a sound like that of a great city's populace welcoming a king on his victorious return from the wars. He looks again, and for a moment he sees a speck that must be the barge, far off on the horizon. Then the spot sails on and disappears, "and the new sun rose bringing the new year."

THE CHARACTERS

Abrosius
The friendly monk to whom Percivale tells the story of the Holy Grail.

Anton
A friend of Uther's who raised and protected Arthur during his childhood. Because he kept the boy's identity a secret, it was later sometimes rumored that he had been Arthur's real father.

Arthur
Son of Uther Pendragon, husband of Guinevere, King of Britain. King Arthur is without question the greatest and most heroic figure in English mythology, and a vast medieval cycle of legend and semi-history is built around him. Although he is not present in all its episodes, Arthur is the central character of the *Idylls,* for his influence is felt everywhere. He is portrayed by Tennyson as the model of human perfection for he possesses all the highest qualities to which any man might aspire.

In the various *Idylls* Arthur is shown in his different aspects. First he is seen as a great warrior; then as a constructive and idealistic statesman. All Arthur's efforts are devoted to the well-being of Britain; because of his deep religious and moral sense, he works ceaselessly to bring the true religion to fruition among his countrymen. Arthur's philosophy of life is most fully embodied in the speech in lines 899-915 of "The Holy Grail."

As the forces of evil gain more strength and begin to exert influence at court, the greatness of Arthur is seen even more clearly. He retains all his personal dignity and majesty, even in the midst of utter chaos and the destruction of all his hopes. In the last half of the poem the King, through his adversities, rises to a high, tragic stature. Even when he learns the awful truth about Guinevere and Lancelot, Arthur is able to be merciful and unselfish.

Arthur's heroic nature and humanity stand out most at the time of his last battle, when he is at last face-to-face with death and the end of his kingdom. To the last he retains his courage and steadfast purpose, and passes over to the mysterious island of Avilion with confidence and faith.

By making Arthur a paragon of human virtue and the embodiment of Victorian morality, Tennyson unfortunately has also made him unreal as a man. He is the weakest character in the poem, for it is impossible to believe in him as a human being. Arthur stands as a magnificent example of what a man might become, but offers little to the reader who seeks to learn what men are. Arthur's presence or behavior in an otherwise dramatic situation often has an air of falsity or didacticism. For example, his final speech to Guinevere is superb in its compassion, but also priggishly intolerable and very like a dull sermon.

Aurelius

One of the predecessors of Arthur. He was able to unite the kingdom for a short time after the Roman army left Britain.

Balan

The brother of Balin.

Balin

Known as "the savage," he is a sensitive and well-intentioned knight, but unfortunately is subject to temporary spells of madness. During one of these fits he kills his beloved brother.

Bedivere

One of Arthur's most loyal followers, he is the first to be knighted by the new King and the only survivor of the last battle. He carries out many important missions for Arthur, including the embassy to ask for the hand of Guinevere, and the final disposal of the sword Excalibur.

Bellicent

The daughter of Gorlois and Ygerne (hence the half-sister of Arthur), wife of King Lot, and mother of Gawain, Modred, and Gareth. In some medieval sources she is also known as Morgan le Fay.

Bors

The nephew of Lancelot. He is among the noblest and most holy of knights, and is one of the few to whom even a fleeting vision of the Grail is allowed.

Carados

One of the enemy kings overcome by Arthur at the start of his reign.

Dagonet

Arthur's court jester, and one of his most loyal servants. He is both a humorous and pathetic character. Despite his position as fool, Dagonet is a sensitive observer of affairs at court, but he is powerless to affect them. He is the only significant figure in the *Idylls* who is completely Tennyson's creation.

Doorm

Known as "the bull," an outlaw earl who leads a band of brigands from his stronghold in Lyonnesse. He is killed by Geraint after having molested Enid.

Dubric

The sainted head of the Church in Britain during the reign of Arthur.

Edyrn, Son of Nudd

Known as "the sparrow-hawk." He is a suitor of Enid, and a haughty knight who unjustly expropriates the holdings of his uncle Yniol. After being chastened by Geraint's defeat of him, he comes under the influence of Dubric and others at the Round Table. Eventually he becomes one of Arthur's noblest and most honorable knights, and loyally dies in the King's service. His story presents an example of Arthur's ideals in action, at a time when decay has not yet eaten into the moral structure at Camelot.

Elaine

The Tennysonian personification of the finest and most admirable virtues of womanhood. She possesses beauty and grace, innocence and goodness, unselfishness and fidelity. Elaine dies of a broken heart when she learns that her love for Lancelot is not answered, but even at the moment of her death she never expresses any bitterness or malice.

Enid

The daughter of Yniol, and wife of Geraint. She is another Tennysonian portrait of an admirable and noble maiden. Enid is most noteworthy for her patience and humility, as well as her unselfish love for Geraint.

Ettarre

In this character Tennyson portrays a wicked woman whose main characteristics are pride, selfishness, and greed. As a result of her cruelty, Pelleas meets his downfall.

Galahad

The personification of perfect purity and innocence, achieved through total renunciation and resistance to temptation. He is the holiest of knights and the only one to be blessed with a complete and permanent vision of the Grail.

Galahad is a saintly character, but has become this through asceticism and withdrawal from the world. As a result, he is a cold person in many respects. He generally seems more concerned with his own salvation than with the welfare and service of humanity, although these last are among the most important aims of Arthur and the Round Table.

In some medieval sources Galahad is reputed to be the illegitimate son of Lancelot and Elaine, but Tennyson specifically denies this in the *Idylls*.

Gareth

Son of Bellicent and Lot, brother of Gawain and Modred. He is Tennyson's picture of the perfect knightly hero, and represents the highest type of true manhood and chivalry. He excels even the saintly Galahad, for the latter possesses none of the warm human qualities that are essential parts of Gareth's nature.

Garlon

Nephew and heir of King Pellam; he has a brief and unpleasant encounter with Balin.

Gawain

Son of Bellicent and Lot, brother of Modred and Gareth. He is one of the most prominent knights at court. Despite the portrayal of him given by Malory and other medieval sources, in the *Idylls* he is seen as a gossip and troublemaker, most renowned for his fickleness, irresponsibility, and facetiousness. His acts in "Lancelot and Elaine" and "Pelleas and Ettarre" provide good examples of this.

Geraint

Prince of Devon, husband of Enid. The most important characteristic of Geraint is his senseless and unfair suspicion of his wife. In the poems about these two, Tennyson studies in depth the consequences of mistrust and lack of communication between lovers. In addition, Geraint's harsh treatment of the innocent Enid provides an interesting contrast with Arthur's generosity to the guilty Guinevere.

Gorlois

Duke of Tintagil, first husband of Ygerne. Because so few were aware of the events that had preceded the death of Uther, it was often rumored that Gorlois had been Arthur's father.

Guinevere

Daughter of Leodogran, wife of Arthur. When Guinevere first appears in the poem, she is characterized by her beauty, womanly strength, and royal dignity. As her sinful love for Lancelot develops, however, she becomes selfish, cruel, and passionate. She is indicated to be the unwitting human cause of the moral ruin that eventually infects and destroys the whole court.

Guinevere has no sympathy for Arthur's ideals and little consideration or affection for him as a man. She is solely concerned with her own interests and her adulterous love for Lancelot; she brazenly conceals this from no one except Arthur. Tennyson's portrayals of evil women, particularly Ettarre, provide deep insights into the character of Guinevere.

It is only near the end of the poem that Guinevere is made aware of the moral consequences of her conduct. She realizes that she has always loved only Arthur, and though it is now too late to amend her past deeds, she repents for her sins, becomes a nun, and devotes her last years to prayers and good works.

Isolt
The wife of King Mark and lover of Tristram; also the daughter of the King of Brittany and wife of Tristram.

Kay
The steward of Arthur's palace. He is narrow-minded, cynical, and intolerant, as is shown by his attitude towards Gareth. In some medieval sources Kay is said to be Arthur's foster-brother.

Lancelot
"The flower of chivalry," he is the greatest of all knights and Arthur's closest friend. He is a noble and honorable man, whose reputation is sullied only by his sinful relationship with Guinevere. Lancelot often feels acute guilt and shame about his adultery and his infidelity to Arthur. He frequently makes strong but unsuccessful efforts to untangle himself from the influence of this evil. Because of the confusing ambivalence between his love for Guinevere and his knightly code of conduct, Lancelot often has spells of extreme depression and self-recrimination. It is because of this one great sin that he is not allowed to see the Grail except through a cloud, even though in all other things he is virtuous. In Lancelot, Tennyson presents a moving portrait of a great soul tortured by a guilty conscience, and struggling manfully to free itself from sin.

Lavaine
One of the brothers of Elaine.

Leodogran
King of Cameliard and father of Guinevere.

Limours

One of the suitors of Enid, he is a coarse drunkard. While they are passing through his earldom, he makes an unsuccessful attempt to steal Enid from Geraint.

Lot

King of Orkney, husband of Bellicent, father of Gawain, Modred, and Gareth. He is one of the allied kings overcome by Arthur in his first major battle.

Lynette

The sister of Lyonors. She is a delightful young maiden. At first, probably because of her youth and lack of experience, she is somewhat proud and overconcerned with social status. From her relationship with Gareth, she learns tolerance and humility, and eventually the two are married.

Lyonors

The sister of Lynette; she is rescued from her captors by Gareth.

Mark

King of Cornwall and husband of Isolt. Mark has always hated and envied Arthur. He is a cowardly and treacherous villain who sends Vivien to undermine Arthur's influence, and who murders Tristram while his victim is defenseless.

Merlin

A great magician and sage, he is Arthur's powerful helper and protector, as well as his friend and adviser. He is an old man, and despite his wisdom is susceptible to Vivien's subtle blandishments. Because of this weakness he is eliminated from Camelot, an action which makes possible the eventual downfall of the King. Merlin is himself the center of an extensive medieval cycle of legends and romances.

Modred

The oldest son of Lot, brother of Gawain and Gareth. He is a sullen, evil, and treacherous knight who continually plots against his King until he is finally able to usurp the throne during Arthur's absence in France. He is killed by Arthur in the last battle, but manages to fatally wound the King in return.

Pellam

One of the kings who opposed Arthur at the start of his reign. Under Arthur's influence he has a spiritual rebirth and becomes a deeply religious man. The spear with which the side of Christ was pierced is the most sacred relic in his private chapel.

Pelleas

An inexperienced and naive young knight who, despite his sincere and honest intentions, is taken advantage of and driven to his downfall by the cruel machinations of Ettarre. The great pain and confusion which Pelleas feels when he learns that all his beliefs about the honor and high ethical standards of the Round Table are false provides a good example of the way in which Guinevere's sin spread to infect others. The waste of such valuable human resources as Pelleas, who compares very favorably at first with Gareth, makes more poignant the tragic downfall of Arthur's regime.

Percivale

The hero of many medieval legends centering around the quest for the Grail, he is the same character as the Parsifal of Wagner's opera and the Peredur of Welsh legend.

When Percivale begins his quest he is confident, for he is filled with false pride in his own achievements. Through his long and fruitless search he ultimately comes to the conviction of his own unworthiness and the knowledge that the things men most covet are mere illusions. From his encounter with the hermit and Galahad he finally learns the meaning of humility. After gaining this new understanding, he is graced with a vision of the Grail. Percivale ends his life as a monk.

Torre

One of the brothers of Elaine.

Tristram

The lover of Isolt. He, like many others in the *Idylls,* is the center of many medieval legends. He appears in "The Last Tournament" as a brazen and self-righteous sinner who has no shame whatsoever for any of his crimes. Because there is such a close similarity between his relationship with Isolt and that of Lancelot with Guinevere (the second Isolt is the double of Elaine), his function here seems to be as a demonstration of the full extent and evil nature of Lancelot's adultery.

Urien

One of the neighboring kings who attacks Leodogran prior to Arthur's coronation.

Uther Pendragon

The father of Arthur. During his lifetime he ruled nearly all Britain, but when he died the kingdom he had built fell apart again. This was because the feudal nobles and tributary kings were eager to reassert their own power, and no one knew that Uther had left an heir.

Vivien

She plays an active part in the undermining and destruction of the moral order at Camelot; she spreads vicious rumors of all kinds, is responsible for the disappearance of Merlin, shares some of the blame for the deaths of Balin and Balan, and aids Modred in the usurpation of the throne. Vivien represents the forces of evil and unrestrained passion as they manifest themselves in the feminine character; she is totally unscrupulous and immoral.

Ygerne

The wife of Gorlois and mother by him of Bellicent. Although she was already married, Uther Pendragon fell in love with her. Ygerne refused his advances and remained faithful to her husband. As a result, Uther went to war with Gorlois, defeated and slew him. Afterwards, Uther besieged and captured Tintagil Castle and forced Ygerne to submit to him. Uther and Ygerne were the parents of Arthur, but Uther died a few months before his son was born. The parentage of the infant was kept a secret in order to protect his life; hence the various rumors about Arthur's "real" father.

Yniol

The father of Enid.

GEOGRAPHICAL NAMES

Almesbury

The site of the abbey where Guinevere takes refuge, located near Salisbury in south-central England.

Astolat

The castle of Elaine's father, located at Guilford in Surrey in southeastern England.

Avilion

Also known as *Avalon.* In Celtic mythology this is the mysterious island paradise to which the dead souls of heroes and the blessed are taken. It is located somewhere in the western sea.

Badon Hill

The site of the last and greatest of Arthur's twelve legendary battles against the heathen.

Brittany

The region in France south of Normandy and opposite southern England. In ancient times it was inhabited by a Celtic people closely related to the Britons (hence its name) and is frequently mentioned in the Arthurian legends.

Broceliande

A forested area in Brittany to which Merlin and Vivien wander.

Caerleon-Upon-Usk

One of the traditional seats of Arthur's court, located near Newport in Monmouthshire on the southwestern coast of England.

Cameliard

The legendary kingdom of Leodogran, location uncertain.

Camelot

The mythical capital of Arthur's kingdom. Its location is uncertain, although various spots have been suggested by scholars, including Winchester, Cadbury Castle near Glastonbury, and several places in Wales.

Cornwall
The kingdom of Mark, located in southwestern England.

Devon
The princedom of Geraint, located in southwestern England.

Glastonbury
The site of an abbey said to have been founded by Joseph of Arimathea at the time of his legendary arrival in Britain, located on the southeastern coast of England.

Lyonnessee
A mythical region supposed to be somewhere near Cornwall; it is mentioned only in the Arthurian romances.

Orkney
The kingdom of Lot, located in northern Scotland.

Tintagil
The dukedom of Gorlois, located in Cornwall.

THE ARTISTRY AND MEANING OF THE *IDYLLS*

The *Idylls of the King* can be approached as a collection of romantic tales of chivalry, recounted in beautiful descriptive lyrics. These poems may also, however, be interpreted as a series of moral allegories, which are bound together in a comprehensive presentation of a spiritual philosophy of life and clothed in the garb of poetic narrative. It was in large part due to the ethical aspects of these poems that the *Idylls* were so highly regarded by Tennyson's contemporaries.

Throughout the *Idylls* it is possible to trace a constantly recurring moral theme — the ruin of a great and noble ideal by the increasing and deepening influence on a single sin, despite the hero's ("the blameless King") innocence.

As a direct result of the unimpeded growth of Guinevere's immorality and the contagious effect of this sin, Arthur's constructive and visionary work is hindered and ultimately destroyed. The *Idylls* of "Balin and Balan" and "Pelleas and Ettarre," as well as several others, offer direct examples of this. Tennyson describes sin as a corrosive entity which has the quality of spreading like a fungus and ruining all it touches, unless it is checked at its source. Just as an illness cannot successfully be cured only by treating one or two symptoms without examining the basic causes, so evil too must be dealt with at its root. Arthur's failure is his inability to visualize or cope with evil in this broad sense; he makes the error of believing that he can build a new moral order on a foundation of immoral people.

The *Idylls* lack the tight unity of an epic poem, but a careful study demonstrates that many apparently independent or unconnected episodes are all related, more or less directly, to this single central theme. The individual poems not only contain interesting stories, but also provide stimulating and provoking insights into this central motif. For example, one is better able to evaluate Arthur's attitude towards Guinevere after observing the very different behavior of Geraint to Enid. The contrasted reactions of Elaine and Guinevere to Lancelot and to each other, and the bold shamelessness of Tristram, among other incidents, contribute to a fuller moral awareness on the part of the reader. Nearly all the episodes and characters in the *Idylls* assist through this counterpoint and contrast in the development of an enlightened and profound understanding of the nature of good and evil.

Moreover, a number of the individual *Idylls* are themselves short moral allegories (*e.g.* "Gareth and Lynette"), each illustrating specific problems or ideas, the sum total of which is to strengthen and affirm the ethical message of the entire poem. Unfortunately, Tennyson's allegory is often vague or too obvious, because it attempts to force the ethical principles of the poet's own era onto legends of a period in which they did not exist. It is only in such a poem as "The Holy Grail," where a moral theme already existed in the legend, that Tennyson's use of allegory is successful and effective.

The central theme of moral decay is emphasized by the chronological aspect of the *Idylls*. It is the gradual change in mood, over a period of time, that provides one of the major connective links of the poems. The action of the *Idylls* follows closely the seasons of the year from springtime to winter. Tennyson makes brilliant use of the symbolism of nature to illustrate his theme. As the year wanes, the mood of the poem becomes less optimistic and more over-shadowed by a sense of doom and foreboding. This reaches its culmination in "Guinevere" and "The Passing of Arthur" where, in the midst of winter, the all-pervading feeling of evil, failure, and desolation is inescapable.

The *Idylls* contain many other ethical and epic elements, most notably in their overall depiction of the heroic battle of a great soul, with noble purposes and ideals, against the overwhelming forces of evil. Arthur's titanic struggle ends in defeat, but this defeat seems only temporary, and there is at least a brief final vision of the ulti-mate triumph of virtue and Arthur's ideals in the new spring yet to come.

The dramatic background to this saga of the conflict between good and evil is the story of the poem's four main characters: Lan-celot, Guinevere, Elaine, and Arthur. The first three are success-fully and distinctly drawn, particularly Lancelot, who presents a magnificent picture of a noble and chivalrous man made captive and ruined by his own passions.

The character of Arthur, though, is a failure, and because of this the entire story has a false and heavyhanded quality. The King, a paragon of human virtue, is in effect made into a symbol instead of a man, and lacks warmth or humanity. It is impossible for read-ers to sympathize with Arthur's plight or to identify with him, except in the most abstract way. Because of this defect in characterization, the very human story of these four people does not evoke any tender human response, and becomes instead a dull tale about stale characters.

The other major flaw of the *Idylls* is that these poems, despite Tennyson's superb mastery of blank verse, are too shallow and weak in their diction and imagery to properly relate a story of grand passion and barbaric splendor like the ancient Arthurian saga. F. L.

Lucas, a prominent British critic, has crystalized this viewpoint as follows:

> The *Idylls of the King* have no epic quality; their very name betrays them—Malory made into "Idylls"!—the spear of Malory's Lancelot twisted into a china shepherd's crook! Where the action of the story should hurry the reader on, Tennyson's style with its slow, over-polished perfectness is always holding him back, always crying, "Stay a moment; I am so beautiful." And as a picture of the real savagery of the Middle Ages, the *Idylls of the King* are about as adequate as a fancy-dress ball or a parish pageant.

Additional criticisms have been made of Tennyson and his work besides those mentioned above. Among other things, he has been accused, with some justice, of intellectual timidity, prissiness in thought and diction, lack of emotional depth, and inability to compose a long narrative. All of these censures have resulted in new evaluations of Tennyson as a poet, and have demonstrated that he is not fully worthy of the high stature once accorded him.

Nevertheless, in certain ways Tennyson was a great poet and in these same ways the *Idylls of the King* is a great poem. Tennyson was extremely talented, and possessed some of the supreme gifts of poetry. He was a truly great stylist and had a masterful flair for descriptive lyrics. He was able to depict scenes from nature with an authenticity and intensity of feeling that may be compared only to that of Vergil. It has been truly said of Tennyson that the background crowns the work, for while his stories or characters may be rapidly forgotten, their settings are remembered forever. Some of the most vivid and consummate passages in the *Idylls* are those which portray the sea or the English coast and countryside. A host of examples will be recalled to the mind of the alert and sensitive reader.

Furthermore, Tennyson's prosody has a rhythmic and metrical precision that has rarely been achieved or duplicated by other poets. As an artist, Tennyson was a perfectionist; he had a superb ear for delicate nuances of sound, a matchless smoothness and purity of diction. His work is outstanding for its technical and stylistic polish. Much of Tennyson's poetry is now considered dated and of little worth, and some of it was never of any real value, but he also composed a number of great poems which are cherished among the treasures of the English literary heritage. F. L. Lucas, in his final evaluation of Tennyson, has said:

> ...after the laughter, there is room, still more, for silent wonder at this master, who, coming so late in our literature, yet made such music, never heard before, and now surely to be heard through the centuries, from the English country and the English tongue —
>
> "Lord over Nature, Lord of the visible earth,
> Lord of the senses five."

(Both the above quotations are taken from F. L. Lucas, *Ten Victorian Poets*, Cambridge University Press, 1948.)

TENNYSON'S LIFE AND WORKS

Alfred Tennyson was born August 6, 1809, in Somersby, Lincolnshire, England, where his father was the rector. He was the fourth of twelve children. Alfred was a bright and talented boy, and the fine physique and manly good looks which characterized him as an adult were noticeable even at an early age.

Until he was eleven, Tennyson attended a grammar school in the nearby town of Louth, of which he later had very unhappy memories. From then on, he remained at home where he studied under the close supervision of his scholarly father. Tennyson demonstrated his literary talents quite early, and by the age of fourteen had written a drama in blank verse and a 6000 line epic poem. He was also interested in the study of science, particularly astronomy and geology. In 1827 a small volume entitled *Poems by Two Brothers* containing works by Alfred and Charles Tennyson, as well as a few short contributions by Frederick Tennyson, was published in Louth.

In 1828 Tennyson matriculated at Trinity College, Cambridge. Despite his intelligence and good looks he was excessively shy and was quite unhappy. After a while, however, he joined an informal club known as "the Apostles" which counted among its members the most outstanding young men at the university. Here he was praised highly for his poetry, and he made the acquaintance of Arthur Henry Hallam, a brilliant young man, who was to become his closest and dearest friend. In 1829 Tennyson won the Newdigate Prize for poetry.

In 1830 while Tennyson was still an undergraduate, his volume *Poems, Chiefly Lyrical* was published, but it made no significant impression of the reading public. That summer he and Hallam went to Spain with the romantic notion of joining a band of insurgents in the Pyrennes. They successfully delivered a large sum of money collected on behalf of the rebels, but there is no record of their having participated in any military engagement. In 1831, after his return, Tennyson was forced to leave the university without taking his degree, due to the death of his father.

Following this, Tennyson lived quietly with his family at Somersby. He spent his time working on his poems and engaging in various outdoor sports and activities. Hallam was engaged to one of Tennyson's sisters and spent a great deal of time at the family home, so that the two young men were able to be together often.

In 1832 *Poems by Alfred Tennyson* was published, in which early versions of many of his finest pieces appeared, including "The Lady of Shalott," "The Palace of Art," "The Lotos-Eaters," "Oenone," and "A Dream of Fair Women." The quality of the poems in the volume was not constant, and many of them were overly sentimental or lacking in polish. As a result, despite the fine lyrics mentioned above, the book received a very harsh critical reaction. Tennyson had never been able to stand criticism of his work, and he was deeply hurt by this. For a long time he wrote nothing at all, but finally resolved to devote himself even more fully to the development of his poetic skill.

In 1833 Hallam died suddenly while in Vienna. The shock of this tragic loss affected Tennyson severely. He withdrew completely from all his usual activities and spent his time in mourning and meditation. During his bereavement he thought often about his affection for Hallam and about such problems as the nature of God and the immortality of the soul. During this long period of anguish and grief, Tennyson composed many very moving elegies and lyrics on the death of his beloved friend. These were eventually collected and published in 1850, and are considered one of the greatest elegaic works in English literature, *In Memoriam: A.H.H.*

During the next few years Tennyson continued to live with his family which had now moved to London, and to apply himself to his studies and writing. He became engaged to Emily Sellwood, despite the objection of her parents, but felt it was impossible for them to marry because his financial resources were so limited. In 1842 a two volume collection of his work appeared, containing many revisions of earlier poems, besides a number of excellent new ones, including "Morte d'Arthur," "Ulysses," and "Locksley Hall." At last Tennyson was recognized as one of the leading literary figures of the period and was acclaimed throughout England.

At this time Tennyson lost his small inheritance through a foolish investment, and sffered a serious nervous breakdown as a result. Upon his recovery he was provided with an annual pension by the British government. In June, 1850, after an engagement of thirteen years, Tennyson and Emily were married. Later that same year Tennyson was appointed to the post of poet laureate, succeeding Wadsworth. Among the most notable poems he wrote while holding that office are the "Ode on the Death of the Duke of Wellington" (1852) and "The Charge of the Light Brigade" (1854).

Despite his fame Tennyson remained shy and moved from London to a more secluded home. He worked intently on his Arthurian poems, the earliest of which had been published in the 1832 volume, and the first four *Idylls* appeared in 1859. These rapidly became his most popular works, and he continued to revise and add to them until the *Idylls of the King* reached its present form in the edition of 1885.

The remainder of Tennyson's life was uneventful. He and Emily had a son, whom they named Hallam. Tennyson was hailed as the greatest of English poets and was awarded numerous honors; he received an honorary degree from Oxford University in 1885, and was offered the rectorship of Glasgow University. In 1883 he was raised to the peerage by Queen Victoria and was thereafter known as Baron Tennyson of Aldworth. He was the first Englishman to be granted such a high rank solely for literary distinction. Among his friends Tennyson counted such noteworthy people as Albert, the Prince Consort, W. E. Gladstone, the prime minister, Thomas Carlyle, the historian, and Edward FitzGerald, the poet.

All his life Tennyson continued to write poetry. His later volumes include *Maude, A Monodrama* (1855), *Enoch Arden* (1864), *Ballads and Poems* (1880), *Tiresias and Other Ballads* (1885), *Locksley Hall Sixty Years After* (1886), *Demeter and Other Poems* (1889), and *The Death of Oenone* (published post-humously in 1892). He also wrote a number of historical dramas in poetic form, among which are *Queen Mary* (1875), *Harold* (1877), *Beckett* (1884), and *The Foresters* (1892).

Alfred Lord Tennyson was the most highly regarded poet of his period and the most widely read of all English poets. The quality of his work varied greatly, and much that he wrote is of little interest today, for he included in his poetry themes and subjects that were of intense interest only to the Victorians. Tennyson's thought was often shallow, and dealt with matters of fleeting significance, but his technical skill and prosody were unsurpassed. Perhaps the most perceptive evaluation of his work is embodied in Tennyson's own remark to Carlyle:

> I don't think that since Shakespeare there has been such a master of the English language as I — to be sure, I have nothing to say.

Tennyson died at Aldworth House, his home in Surrey, on October 6, 1892, at the age of eighty-four. He was buried in the Poet's Corner at Westminster Abbey, and the copy of Shakespeare's play *Cymbeline* which he had been reading on the night of his death was placed in his coffin.

THE ARTHURIAN LEGENDS

The tales about King Arthur and the knights of the Round Table, from which Tennyson drew the inspiration and substance of his *Idylls,* form an extensive body of medieval literature. The Arthurian legends have always had a firm hold on the English imagination, due to the heroic and evocative picture of the British past which they present. Tennyson was under great pressure to compose a long poem on an epic theme, and it was only natural for him to have selected as his subject the figure who would arouse strong sentiments of patriotism, pride, and admiration in the hearts of all Englishmen.

There is practically no historical evidence about the real King Arthur. It is considered probable, however, that he was a minor king or war-leader of the Celtic Britons who, sometime in the fifth of sixth century A.D., led his people in a stubborn and temporarily successful resistance against the Anglo-Saxon invasion. Despite Arthur's legendary twelve battles, culminating in the great victory at Mount Badon, the Anglo-Saxons were ultimately triumphant and drove the defeated Britons into the remote regions of Scotland and Wales. It was in these areas that the Arthurian legends first arose.

Whoever Arthur was, and whatever his real achievement, there is no question that he rapidly became the most important hero and the central figure of British legendary history. It is considered likely that many ancient Celtic myths and traditions became attached to his name. Furthermore, as time passed, various other legendary figures such as Gawain, Bedivere, Lancelot, and Tristram, who had once all been independent, became secondary to Arthur in the later versions of the sagas. Arthur's fame was widespread, and early legends about him are reported from such diverse areas as Brittany, Cornwall, Wales, Cumberland, and Scotland. By the end of the Middle Ages, he was the hero of romances composed even in France, Germany, Italy, and Spain.

The earliest documentary account of Arthur is found in the *Historia Britonum* composed by the Welsh Nennius (*fl.* 796). The first important extended description of Arthur's career is in the

Historia Regium Britanniae written by Geoffrey of Monmouth about 1140, although it has been suggested that the author actually invented many of the incidents he reports. Additional personal and historical details are found in the *Annales Cambriae* (*c*. 954), the Norman-French version of Geoffrey's *Historia* composed by Wace (1155), the *Gesta Regum Anglorum* written by William of Malmesbury in 1125, the chronicle of Layamon (early 13th century), as well as a few other Welsh and English sources.

In addition to these pseudo-historical accounts, there were from the earliest times a large number of bardic songs and lays dealing with a host of characters and events from the now extensive Arthurian saga. A great number of these derive from the Welsh tradition. These are thought to be among the most important sources since Arthur was supposed to have been the leader of the Celtic Britons from whom the Welsh are descended. The most considerable collection of these Welsh legendary tales is kown as the *Mabinogion*. The oldest poems in this collection have been attributed to the 6th century A.D. This date may be questionable, but the *Mabinogion* definitely contains many primitive elements and was certainly composed in a very early period.

Later in the Middle Ages, elaborate and cultivated forms of metrical and prose romances were developed, and Arthurian themes provided the most popular subject matter. The rough basic material of the legends was softened and polished by exposure to the new literary conventions of chivalry and courtly love.

The most well-known of the Arthurian metrical romances are those composed by the French poet, Chretien de Troyes (*fl.* 1160-1185). The greatest and most famous of the Arthurian prose romances is the *Morte D'Arthur* of Sir Thomas Malory (published 1485). This is the most thorough and complete redaction of the legends and the one from which Tennyson drew most of his material. It is also judged to be one of the finest romantic works in English literature.

The student will find a complete and unified account of all the Arthurian legends in a highly readable form in *The Age of Chivalry*

by Thomas Bulfinch. This classic is currently available in a paperback edition.

SUGGESTIONS FOR ADDITIONAL READING

Baum, P.F. *Tennyson Sixty Years After*. Chapel Hill, N.C., 1948.

Bulfinch, Thomas. *The Age of Chivalry*. New York, 1962 (paperback).

Killham, J., ed. *Critical Essays on the Poetry of Tennyson*. London, 1960.

Lucas, F. L. *Tennyson* ("Writers and their Work" series pamphlet
no. 83). London, 1957 (paperback).

_____. *Ten Victorian Poets*. Cambridge, Eng., 1948.

Littledale, H. *Essays on Idylls of the King*. London, 1893.

Nicholson, Harold. *Tennyson: Aspects of his Life, Character, and
Poetry*. London, 1923.

Tennyson, Hallam. *Alfred, Lord Tennyson: A Memoir*. London,
1897.

Tennyson, Charles. *Tennyson*. London, 1949.

Untermeyer, Louis. *Lives of the Poets*. New York, 1961.

SAMPLE EXAMINATION QUESTIONS

1. Analyze the character of King Arthur as he appears in the
   Idylls and discuss whether he is an adequate hero for this
   poem.

2. Compare the characterizations of Guinevere and Elaine.

3. Analyze and discuss the personality of Lancelot.

4. Discuss the central moral theme of the *Idylls* and the relation to this of the separate poems in the collection.

5. Explain the use of allegory and symbolism in the *Idylls*.

6. Compare the personalities of Percivale and Galahad, and discuss the religious message of "The Holy Grail."

7. What are the main strengths and weaknesses of Tennyson as a poet? Refer in your answer to various aspects of the *Idylls*.

8. Describe the "historical" King Arthur and the development of the Arthurian legend.

9. Give a brief account of Tennyson's place in English literature, mentioning his other major works.

10. Explain Tennyson's conception of sin as it is presented in the *Idylls*.

11. Compare the two *Idylls*, "The Coming of Arthur" and "The Passing of Arthur" in terms of mood and function, making reference to imagery, diction, and other forms of prosody.

12. Identify the following minor characters, stating briefly their roles in the *Idylls*: Enid, Gareth, Tristram, Dagonet, Merlin, Balin, Modred, Bellicent, Geraint, Bedivere, Vivien, Pelleas, Gawain, and Ettarre.

NOTES

NOTES

NOTES

NOTES

NOTES

NOTES